RS. 2/2015

RHYTHMIC GYMNASTICS

LET'S DANCE

Tracy M. Maurer

The Rourke Press, Inc.
Vero Beach, Florida 32964

Tracy M. Maurer, author of the Dance Series, specializes in non-fiction and business writing. She has previously worked with several educational organizations on various writing projects, including creating classroom workbooks for elementary students. Tracy's most recently published hard cover book focused on the city of Macon, Georgia. A graduate of the University of Minnesota - Minneapolis School of Journalism, she now lives in Park Falls, Wisconsin, with her husband Mike.

PHOTO CREDITS
© Timothy L. Vacula: cover, pages 7, 8, 10, 12, 15, 17, 18, 21; © Lois M. Nelson: title page; © Tracey Callahan Monar: pages 4, 13

EDITORIAL SERVICES:
Penworthy Learning Systems and Lois M. Nelson

With appreciation to Nora Campbell, USA Gymnastics, Indianapolis, IN; Cindy Bickman, Chattooga Gym, Marietta, GA; Marina Gladkova, The Rhythmic Gymnastics Center, Minneapolis, MN

Library of Congress Cataloging-in-Publication Data

Maurer, Tracy, 1965-
   Rhythmic Gymnastics / Tracy M. Maurer.
      p. cm. — (Let's dance)
   Includes index
   Summary: Covers the history and techniques of and competitive events in the sport of rhythmic gymnastics.
   ISBN 1-57103-171-5
   1. Rhythmic Gymnastics—Juvenile literature. [1. Rhythmic gymnastics. 2. Gymnastics] I. Title II. Series: Maurer, Tracy, 1965- Let's dance.
GV463.M35 1997
796.44—dc21   97–8394
                                                                          CIP
                                                                           AC

Printed in the USA

TABLE OF CONTENTS

RHYTHMIC GYMNASTICS

Rhythmic gymnastics mixes music, dance, and athletic skills to form one of the world's most beautiful sports. It borrows many graceful movements from ballet dancing. Rhythmic gymnasts even walk high on their toes, or on **half-toe** (HAF toh), almost like ballerinas.

Ballet makes up just one part of this sport. Rhythmic gymnasts learn the floor acrobatics that **artistic gymnasts** (ahr TIS tik JIM nasts) perform. They also master moving with five different **apparatus** (AP uh RAT us): rope, hoop, ball, clubs, and ribbon.

Rhythmic gymnastics classes begin with exercises to warm up the muscles; the gymnasts move as gracefully as ballerinas.

THE APPARATUS

The apparatus make rhythmic gymnastics exciting to watch. **Spectators** (SPEK TAY turz) especially like the snake-like shapes of the long ribbons.

Juggling, bouncing, waving, tossing and catching, or other tricks with the apparatus demand fine athletic skills. Each apparatus feels different because of its shape, and switching from one to another is difficult. Gymnasts usually use four apparatus in each competition. The hardest trick is to make it look easy!

Judges check the gymnasts' apparatus before each competition to be sure all of the equipment meets strict standards.

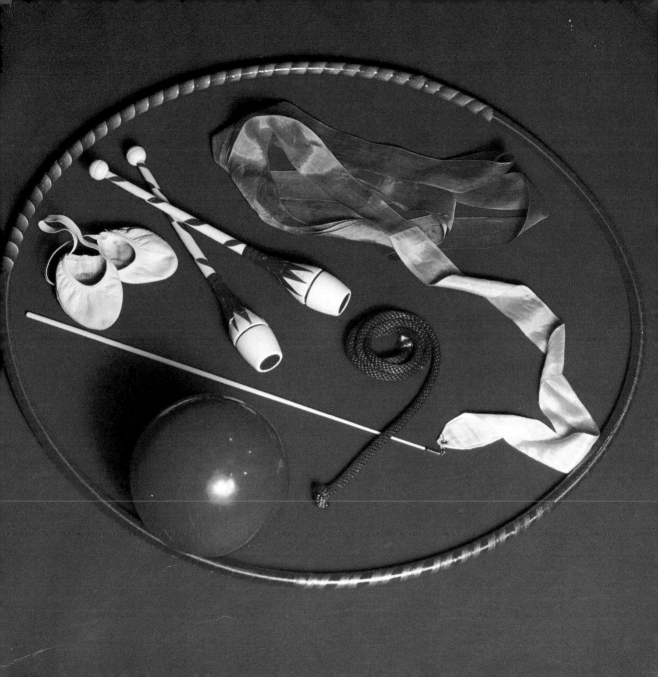

A BLEND OF SKILLS

The ancient Greeks believed that exercise joined the mind with the body. "Gymnastics" comes from their word for exercises.

Rhythmic gymnastics began in Sweden in the 1800s. It still blends skills of the mind and body. Gymnasts work for strong and flexible muscles to leap and bend easily. They also need balance to hold positions.

Rhythmic gymnasts make even difficult positions for handling the apparatus look easy and graceful.

MOVING TO THE MUSIC

Rhythmic gymnasts often take extra classes in ballet or other kinds of dance. Dance lessons help them learn to move with confidence and grace.

Rhythmic gymnastics coaches **adapt** (uh DAPT) steps from ballet, jazz, and folk dances to create new routines. The music usually matches the dance style.

Coaches know that each routine's **choreography** (KAWR ee OG ruh fee) must include certain movements, such as jumps and turns. The coaches also plan how the gymnasts will move with the apparatus to win the judges.

A coach works with a gymnast to develop a routine.

Rhythmic gymnasts practice every movement in each routine many times to master the proper form.

A rhythmic gymnast may toss the apparatus high into the air, perform a carefully timed movement, and then catch the apparatus as part of her routine.

SOLO AND GROUP ROUTINES

The competitions, or meets, include both solo and group events. Each group competes twice at a meet. In one routine, all five team members use the same type of apparatus. In the other, three use one kind of apparatus and two use another. They exchange the apparatus in both routines. Hundreds of hours of practice allow them to trade off the apparatus with awesome precision.

Group rhythmic gymnastics earned medals for the first time at the 1996 Olympic Games.

Rhythmic gymnastics builds team spirit; two girls help each other stretch their muscles to gain strength and flexibility.

WHAT GYMNASTS WEAR

Most gymnasts wear sleeveless practice **leotards** (LEE uh TAHRDZ) and warm-up shorts. The clothes fit tightly to allow the coach to watch for proper body positions.

Gymnasts compete in long-sleeved leotards or **unitards** (YOO ni TAHRDZ). Often, all the gymnasts from one gym or school dress in special matching "team leos."

The soft leather gymnastics shoes cover only the toes because these athletes perform their routines high on half-toe. Their heels rarely touch the floor.

A rhythmic gymnast tries to keep her apparatus in motion at all times.

LEARNING THE SPORT

Artistic gymnastics became popular in the United States in the 1970s and rhythmic gymnastics gained popularity later. Currently, only girls compete in rhythmic gymnastics.

Girls may start using the apparatus at about three years of age. In the United States, beginners move from Level 1 through Level 10, also called the **elite** (eh LEET) level. The National Team, the next highest level, represents the United States at international competitions.

Classes always seem exciting even for top gymnasts, because the sport requires many different skills.

THE REWARDS OF PRACTICE

The elite routines last about 90 seconds each. It takes hours of practice every day for many years to turn those seconds into a championship performance. Elite gymnasts still go to school or study with a **tutor** (TOO tur) while they train. Sometimes they move away from home to work with certain coaches.

Of course, not everyone becomes a world-class competitor. Most girls join a gym just for fun. They enjoy learning the dance-like moves and using the different apparatus. They make new friends, too.

The sport develops concentration, creativity, teamwork, and athletic skills that the athletes will use throughout their lives.

WHERE TO SEE RHYTHMIC GYMNASTICS

Rhythmic gymnasts of all levels compete at several local or regional meets during the year. The elite and National Team gymnasts compete at many national and international events. Every competition welcomes spectators.

Live **exhibitions** (EK suh BISH unz) help show the sport to more people. Sometimes you can see rhythmic gymnastics on television. Libraries, the Internet, and sources such as USA Gymnastics in Indianapolis can also help you learn more about this graceful sport.

Glossary

adapt (uh DAPT) — to change something to fit one's needs

apparatus (AP uh RAT us) — the five objects used in rhythmic gymnastics: hoop, rope, ball, ribbon and clubs

artistic gymnasts (ahr TIS tik   JIM nasts) — athletes who perform acrobatic movements, such as aerials and handsprings, to music in various events

choreography (KAWR ee OG ruh fee) — the planned dance-like steps and movements of a rhythmic gymnast's routine

elite (eh LEET) — the top group of people; in rhythmic gymnastics, the tenth level of competition

exhibitions (EK suh BISH unz) — a show for the public that is not competitive

half-toe (HAF toh) — walking, running, jumping, or other movements using only the ball and toes of the foot

leotards (LEE uh TAHRDZ) — skin-tight, one-piece clothing

spectators (SPEK TAY turz) — the people who watch an event

tutor (TOO tur) — a person who teaches one or a few students, usually a private instructor

unitards (YOO ni TAHRDZ) — one-piece outfits, usually with long-sleeves and leggings, that fit very tightly

INDEX